the sea refus~~~~ river

by Betha~

To:

Pauline

Thanks for supporting!

Bethany
Innes x.

First published 2019 by Fly on the Wall Poetry Press

Published in the UK by
Fly on the Wall Poetry Press
56 High Lea Rd
New Mills
Derbyshire
SK22 3DP

www.flyonthewallpoetry.co.uk

ISBN: 978-1-9995986-5-5

978-1-9995986-5-5

A CIP Catalogue record for this book is available from the British
Library.

These poems are dedicated to anyone who has lost a parent in their childhood:

May you know that you're always loved.

May you find the guides you need to help you through your journeys of grief.

May you find your voice of truth to speak your story, to be heard, to be witnessed, and find the healing you need.

Praise for 'the sea refuses no river'

"There is something of the startled deer in the vulnerable poignancy of these poems. The poems are carefully held in check from being too raw by the references to nature: 'the quiet hills'/ 'a pigeon on a sunlit gate'. This finely exercised restraint lends to these poems a great delicacy and beauty. A fine collection."

- Gill McEvoy

"Bethany Rivers is unusual in contemporary British poetry because she has evolved a discursive mode which allows her to speak explicitly about emotions and (even more unusually) ideas. That is a sign of her powerful personal investment in what she writes and her determination to make poetry speak about important questions – she refuses to write easy conventional poems. These qualities, combined with her ransacking of the everyday for signs of the archetypal, single her out as a poet who deserves to be widely read and thought about."

- Ian Gregson, Professor at Bangor University

Contents

The Gate at Shrewsbury

I'd never noticed before: at the other side
of the tracks a sunbeam falls through
a half open iron gate, not one you'd
expect in a station; iron swirls of infinity
dance on top of the vertical rails, something
you might see at the end of a long drive of
a stately home. I'm on the other side
in the shade of the cooling day, in the wings.

There's still a hectic in my blood of Edinburgh Fringe,
the last three days of it: raucous street theatre, ghost trails,
baristas and barmaids of Europe & South America,
the actors & writers, the talent & hopefuls,
the audiences & ticket sellers, the rounds of applause,
show after show, where each of us goes, seeking
a mirror of nature in the gesture of a character.

I found one of my mirrors. I cracked. I'm grateful.

After seven hours of trains, the quiet hills
of Wales, wait in all their earth-bound patience,
whispering in a wind voice I can never quite
catch. And in the middle of Wales, where sheep
out-number the people, the old fear creeps nearer
waiting to enter my veins: the lost mirror.

A wood pigeon alights on a sunlit wrought iron gate.

Violets – withered all when my father died.

She was born with the language of flowers
though nobody believed her.
Kind of redundant in an age of reason.

A woman drowning amidst the beauty
of summer. Not really. It was the water
of their lies: dead men's fingers; the long purples.

Everywhere she went that same image
followed her, haunted her. On posters, stickers,
paintings, photoshopped pictures.

She read and re-read the play, saw many
performances in French, Polish, Welsh.
The message was still lost. Something

about rosemary. She had fallen in love
once. It had cost her. She spent years
befriending the river: it was her only escape.

At my father's grave

I gaze to the far end of the cemetery
watch naked fronds of a weeping willow
gentle a breeze over the bench
where we never sat together.

My feet feel cold in the fading yellow
leaves folded into your grave.
I'm not really in the coffin, you know.
Then, really, where are you?

Look behind the stone.
I shuffle forwards and look down.
Snowdrops peeping
above the frosted ground.

Hiraeth

Zeina Hashem Beck

Home is not where you think it is, nor is it where
you remember: it's not bricks & mortar
or the place where your parents reside;
some say home is a memory you keep
locked in your heart, but you continuously lose
the key; some say home is the time before
you were born & the time after you die; some say
home is the body you perspire in; some say home
is the hara, the seat of the soul. Love songs declare
home is in the eyes of your lover, or the resonance
of his voice. But I say Home is in the act
of writing. Home is a recitation of Persian poetry,
though you don't understand a word. Home is
in the eyes of a golden statue of Buddha
in a foreign land. Home is in the smell of garlic
on your fingers, three days after you cooked
the curry. Home is a song you keep on losing,
keep hoping to remember.

Shape of Loss

desert as wide as twenty-eight years
wind-swept sand dunes background to

studies, graduation, marriage
cycling, rock climbing, badminton

divorce, friendships found,
friendships broken, seasons

out of kilter, six seasons in one day,
none of the men I've kissed

ever saw the smiling daughter
holding hands with her father

these desert days I carried
the desert flowers forgotten

How to cross the desert

(Based on a Sufi story)

The puddle asked the shepherd
how to cross the desert –
he cupped her in his hands
but she fell through his fingers

The puddle asked the camel
how to cross the desert –
he said he would carry her
but she slipped off his back

The puddle asked the cactus
how to cross the desert –
he said he would drink her
so she sped away

Then she asked the wind
and he said
let yourself evaporate

Seeker

the self that's dying in this
dusty wilderness of no-love

like a cloud that's forgotten
how to rain

my feet are sore
from disconnection

I come to the stems & roots
of the yellow rose

just by the back door
in the garden

frost at its feet
slivers of sun glance

from its thorns
drops of petals & leaves

it looks like gorse in winter
but blooms yellow

in summer, exhales
the scent of honey

I want to know what
the roses know

Deep Fire

My tribe encircle me with drumming, foot-stomping,
chanting & ululating.

heart beats
ancient
as Africa

Their voices swell, undulate, ebb, then build again; to mirror
& uphold my dance. I sway and writhe, make love to the earth.

my hands
hold my hips
like a lover

My body connects to the spaces between us. Their body of music
know who I am.

your heart is
my heart
is your heart

It's not about the broccoli

I never saw you cut broccoli. I didn't know
what you did with the main thick stem. I don't
know if you ever called them fairy trees.

Or how small or how tall you'd cut them.
I don't even know if you liked broccoli,
or whether your body needed the alkaline,

if you ever watched it boil or
timed it steaming and wondered
about whether to, if, maybe, perhaps

and how to, make a cheese sauce, or
would it be al dente next to the carrots,
lamb & mint and new potatoes? Perhaps

you never ate broccoli at all. But as you
watch me now, chop up little green trees
and little green stems, I think of

the home I once knew.

Within

Syria within me
your crumbling empty houses
a skeleton of a city
desolate desecrated
apocalyptic

Palestine within me
your land robbed
olive trees poisoned
crimes against The Wall
barriered bombed broken

Europe within me
every flag of every nation
long peace cross-bordered
patchwork of language & culture
wind carries translations

Blood battles within me
the silent ones that nobody speaks of
in families, out of families, cut between classes
scars and fences needing to be undone
for many generations yet to come

Russian pogroms within me
in the bones of my Great Grandmother
her silent screams from the Pale of Settlement
broken babies
sunset bleeding on the streets

This thirst within me
a desert of carcases
sand-cleaned
stooped against Sahara winds
out-stretched hands

As within, so without

The lawn is tired of green
trying on more faded colours
scraps of straw
barely holding
onto Earth.

Moors blaze their signature.
Hills send smoke signals.
Fields crack open
their own Braille.

Day after day, week after week,
bikinis, shorts, traffic haze & sweat.

But when the moon arrives
in her song of eclipse,
it is cool and clouded.

When heat returns
with teeth, we recede
to the shadows
to breathe.

But when the Earth intercepts
the flow of the Perseids,
our breath can be seen
smudging the outlines
of our shivers. Then
nothing more, nothing
but clouds clouding in upon clouds.

When all the wishes
remain unwished,
the new sickled moon
peers down at us,
wondering when.

It's the colour

you wrap yourself in
comfort blanket when you're dying
inside & you think no-one understands

it's the colour of infinity
so big you turn from it
squint your eyes to a slit

the colour you hadn't expected
fragrant mountain air
so fresh so ancient

you weren't there when I
called your name or
I called the wrong one

but I needed to hear my
name on your lips before I knew
language existed

but it never transpired
I've been thirsting for that
colour my whole life long

Your Map
(After Louise Glück)

Destinations are unclear and million-fold. I have to find 'end'
on the map. It's usually another beginning. A solitary 'A'
of not knowing, trying to find its own Z, when I hear my father's
voice:
my death is not your map, you have to find your own key.

I'm heading for the centre, I think – or is that where I begin?
The centre doesn't feel real at all. You can't see the centre
of an unclear destination. Through a door of star magnolia flowers,
there is life. I hear pigeons coo, full throated. They carry meaning.
They know me well. They're here to guide. They know I'm still stuck
at A.

Out on the winding roads of Wales, there are no memories of you.
That photo you took back in '62, before I was born, that
fountain
which knew you by depth and by blueness, future voices hidden deep.
You passed your camera onto me. You passed on your love of blue.

I call 'Dad'. I call louder. In my dreams I'm always calling you.
New empty houses, derelict streets, me flying above you, & you
occasionally
call back to me through dreams. I don't always know what you mean.

I stare down alleyways, hallways, seaways of azure.
Remember, you say, beneath the desert there is treasure: there is
water.

You & I are always the same distance
(After Rebecca Perry / Zeina Hashem Beck)

The kind of balance between the outward push of heat, its
sky flaring spirals, and the inward pull of gravity has been,
is, the defining law of my universe. That said, a daughter left
without a father, that portrait of grief never framed, gravity
sucks inwards time, blackness, the end of a line. The silence
between stars is like the distance between us.

Silence. A false silence. When fire pulls me inwards how
can I break free? How can a daughter learn to be?
Could she travel years, miles, countries, grief, in a straight
line? Almost never. As fire knows, these are cycles.
Topple the pyres, implode that star, let the heart succumb.
It could go on ad infinitum, this old street.

When you can't measure the distance between stars
and hearts, cut your own heart out, feed it
to the eagle or buzzard. Industry is nothing
but a modern vulture curving its beak
around our throats. Your heart is potent, like
a pomegranate seed, and boundless like a black-time road.

February

February is a plank of wood
between darkest winter and the beginning.

You can be forgiven for
not looking down as you crawl along,

pushing your candle slowly out in front,
your scarf of many colours double-layered.

A survival month: the well is still
empty, and you've yet to find the food

that nourishes. The plank is narrow
and stretches across streams and grass-lands

your feet dare not touch. The plank
is slippery: your hands grip both sides,

sliding one in front of the other,
one in front of the other.

Rise

When you fall down, fall down to your knees,
bent over double, on the bedroom floor,
the bed too far to crawl to,
sun, shadow, rain or snow
makes no difference to your splintering
stomach, the tsunami in your head,
what is it, tell me, what is it
that gets you on your feet again,
what is it that stops you going down
to the river with stones in your pockets?

I ask you this six months later, sitting
on a stool at your kitchen counter, as you percolate
coffee in the dim glow of your sanctuary. This is
the room you love most, brown walls, old signs
from the 1940s, crates nailed to the walls,
silver pans hanging in size order. I know
you've been there. I know you've got up
off the floor. Tell me.

What you say next offers no comfort at all.
Though you want to: your oil lamp isn't bright
enough to light the depths of my well.

I'm a single person, in the world, thirsty.
You're a single mother, with a thread
to the future. You have no choice.

holding the throat
(after Tishani Doshi)

of life a little too tightly the gasping grasping writhing – did you
know the suicidal amongst us are the most thirsty? – holding the
throat where the voice springs from   where the song wants to be-
come   where the voice is throttled down into submission   your
hands whose hands around your own throat whose hands

the voice squeaks becomes tiny   even a mouse roars in comparison;
throat of life –
the shining spinning turquoise sphere of creation   that holds and
keeps on creating
tending towards silence

within that silence is the anticipated birth of something   if only you
could locate the throat
of life   live in it   be in its song   fill the sky the flute the Japanese
wooden flute the wood of many trees gone by   remembering bird
song they used to know

how you wish to fly in that song   but as we all know there is the bass
of the heartbeat tying us to earth and there's the scratch of nails
down blackboards in the back of our minds
that we feign indifference to   or turn up the volume on a dreamer's
speech or dance

like a tribe around a fire of long ago deep to the African beat we're
always longing
to return to but don't know it   the scratching remains of all the bits
of pain you want to
forget but it has just as much right to live to sing as any other part of
you

Destination Overload

and that finally knowing this
you let go and discover that
time is backwards and you were
right all along and that
Ithaca is not what you think
it is, and although the
pain sometimes freezes the
horror in your mind, it
is the journey that carries
the meaning and not
when you arrive

If all the children came out,

                                        if they
came out from behind their computers
and their parents' fears, if they came out
into a large field, dotted by ancient oaks,
if they came out onto football pitches
and playgrounds, with megaphones,
cameras, amplifications of both sight
and sound, if they could record a message,
their own message, to the world, if they came
out and held hands in a ring-a-roses around
the dying olive trees of Palestine, if they came
and camped out on the lawn in front
of the white house and hunger striked,
refused to move, if they remember the
body memory of student protests
in other times and other places, if
they'd seen Tiananmen Square, if they
were allowed to see it, if they knew
that such voices in the world were needed,
encouraged, depended upon, if the children
could come out and hold hands in a long, long
line of song, dancing across and between the
Mexican border, children of all nationalities,
all ages, and sing songs in each other's
languages, as music knows only the language,
of the heart, if all the children could
come out and claim their voices, their heritage,
would we hear them? – would we stop them?
– would we sing with them?

life-song

(after Rumi)

there's a life-song inside every human being
a song inhabited by all your life experiences
this song inside you dying to be heard
you don't know what exactly this song is

sometimes you catch a note of it
a line or a phrase that lives in
someone else's song
you feel the chime of it in your chest

sometimes the song seems to disappear
quiet like stars reflected in a lake
sometimes it's clamouring cathedral bells
ripping rejoicing roaring through the

ordinary tapestry of life the one you
should never believe in and sometimes
it's a thread that runs neatly alongside
someone else's thread wanting to

belong to it and journey together forever
but their thread inevitably departs to some
other part of some other world and you lose
the refrain lose the context and it's hard

to believe in your own life-song again
quiet as the lake without ripples without stars
but there's something that calls something calling you on
as everyone knows song is made of breath

and breath is always there ready within you
to find its own flute
to play like a reed
in the wind

The Stream

You can always be heard
but are not ever seen.
A boy can point to it, name it,
but that's not you.

Your whole journey can be heard
but is never seen.
A boy can glimpse a sunlight reflection
or a fallen shadow.

You know the earth more intimately
than any of us ever will.
A boy draws a line on a map
to symbolise you.

You offer everything and ask for nothing,
yet you are so abused, taken for granted.
A boy learns to float, swim,
build bridges and boats.

You are the veins of hope
greening the land.
A boy may sip, boil, cup, sprinkle,
but cannot keep.

A girl sits on a forest track
she's never met, in a land
she wasn't born in, listens to you say
all the things she's always known.

No voice
(After Rebecca Perry / Zeina Hashem Beck / Seni Seneviratne)

You, with no voice under an aching blue sky, devoid
of the lift of honey, flights of bees, Easter Sunday, violets.
Your mythology is crazed in pavings of
empty chocolate eggs. You crave fire. Flame
the glass of night. It belongs to the phoenix of the mountains.

Fill the glass with broken dreams. Have
it over ice with a blood red straw broken
with hopes that were never described. You see through
the mirror your own invisibility: the silk veil reflecting
broken sunshine, caught on the rocks.

Night is the only true drink and you drink it down
greedily & too soon for too long. Don't.
It won't heal you like that. You know
like the moon knows its orbit
how black the early hours of the mind are.

You tongued the engraving of his name. He stole the food
of your mind. The energy and strength of it. The egg of it.
But dark is a thing that learns how to grow from within. You're
that close to being defeated by your own words. Bottle happy

lingers on your tongue, makes fools of us all
for on that very day, the voices of the dead flare. Listen.
Your breath in the wings of a butterfly, lips that thirst
& crack & wait for gentle things.

tea and buttered toast
(After Rebecca Perry & Jonathan Safran Foer)

all the beaches with their sandy beating hearts:
time the pauses between waves,
 in / out / in /out / in / out
waving tea under your nose like your mother used to

I like eating butterfly buns on the beach,
on a buttered beach with sandwiches
made by your freckled hand,
toast rising on buttered fingers

from my plate to your mouth
from in the depths of your heartbeats
a the / a the / a the / a the
I want the last word to be tamed

I is / I am / I is / you is / you are
you wanted to be enough,
not be more, not be all there is,
just to have enough butter on –

Nameless Now
(after Mary Oliver)

though I will not ever
    know your spoken name as
        it cannot be spoken

I don't know the name you
    truly know me by unless
        it's the one you almost chose

a name can mean so much
    & like an alethiometer
        we don't usually see

deeper meanings the way moonbeams
    penetrate the undergrowth which only
        badgers can see the colours of

though I may not ever know the
    true meaning of how I belong
        to you until after I've given

up this mortal clothing as I learn to live with
    the questions live with the journey
        I'm so often too tired to pursue

but thankfully you come to me
    in dreams & carry that which I cannot
        name or touch to somewhere

where truth is a welcome embrace
    raindrops fall into a forest pond
        the non-words spoken

Every garden is a gift

(Inspired by Grace Cossington Smith's Interior with wardrobe mirror)

You said, I have nothing to say, except bring me love.
I never forgot that night. It was the night before you died.

silence
falls
like petals

There are clothes in the wardrobe now, books on the shelf.
This can only mean, I've moved in, finally.

a book
is a home
you return to

Outside the sun shines. The window & mirror combine
to bring the sunshine in. The garden captured, perfectly framed
in the wardrobe mirror.

no body now
only a frame
your eyes closed

I turn to the daffodils

along the verge of the farm-track
the sunshine they've sucked up and accumulated all spring
how they shine it back on the greyest of days

even clouds have no definition   daffodils torch my thoughts
how I want to be like them consumed by
and shining out my own sunshine

instead of being a swamp who's forgotten her words
there's the occasional caw of crow
but the cows are quiet and still

it's a Sunday a death-day
too much solitude or too much family
or too much dread of Monday morning

the daffodils' delicate musk vanished
with yesterday's sun   I bend to them
turn my face into their yellowness the only colour

alive in the depth of grey   I bend the stalk
near the bottom and hear the break of it
between my finger and thumb

lift it heavenward view it against
the blanket of grey and my hand
heats up   gets hotter and hotter and hotter

the flame of the sun ebbs from the daffodil
into my hand along my wrist up my forearm
along my upper arm rounds-out my shoulder

creeps along my veins to the heart
punishes me with blinding heat   I drop the daffodil
fall to my knees weep with no tears the aching ache

I have been burned. I am glad.

Seven full stops

Some people speak with no
full stops and they build half
walled mazes with crashing paths
never finishing
a sentence or

When my father completed
his full stop I learnt
how to change it
into an ellipsis or a dash...
ignoring
the question mark,
hanging on to the comma –

Jack used full stops
but would erase
them as soon as they hit
the page
I never knew
which statements were true
at any given time

Virginia Woolf sentences seem to run as far as possible
for as long as possible with as many phrases as can
possibly be daisy-linked together before eventually
finally
arriving at that longed for
full stop

If I was a full stop I would be
pink on Mondays and blue
on Sundays

I keep trying to full stop but
the comma keeps
lending its tail

Perhaps the full stop is nothing
but a beautiful
mesmerising circle

Earth sun moon
endlessly full
never stopping

A thank you:

Many thanks to my editor, Isabelle, for believing in this project and being a joy to work with. Thanks to Phillip Gross, Jean Sprackland and James Sheard for their inspiring workshops, where some of these poems were born. Special thanks to Gill McEvoy, Ian Gregson, Graham Hartill, Victoria Field, David Bingham, Robert Harper and my local Stanza group, Deborah Alma, Pat Edwards, Susan Caroline, Eric Ngalle Charles and Mike for their ongoing support and for believing in my work. Thanks to Michele Asbury for her deep understanding. Thanks to my lovely H-family (you know who you are). And thanks to my mum for all her support.

Acknowledgements:

Thanks also to the editors of the following publications where some of these poems or other versions of them have previously appeared: *Three Drops from a Cauldron, I am not a silent poet, Envoi, Hiraeth Erzolirzoli: A Wales/Cameroon Anthology, High Green Dawn, Verve Poetry Press, Writers' Cafe*

Author Biography:

Bethany Rivers' debut pamphlet, *Off the wall,* was published by Indigo Dreams Publishing. She is the author of *'Fountain of Creativity: ways to nourish your writing'* from Victorina Press. Her biggest passions in life are writing and enabling others to write.

She has been widely published in magazines, anthologies and online in the UK and USA, including: *Envoi, Cinnamon Press, Bare Fiction, Fair Acre Press, Verve Poetry Press, Yorkshire Valley Press, Silver Birch Press, The Lampeter Review, The Lake, Blithe Spirit, High Window Literary Journal, Laldy Scottish Literary Journal, Writers' Cafe, Riggwelter, I am not a silent poet, Picaroon Poetry, Three Drops from a Cauldron, The Ofi Press.*

She has an M.A. in Creative Writing from Cardiff University and has taught creative writing for over 13 years. She also mentors writers individually, through the writing of their novels, short stories, children's fiction, memoirs, and poetry: www.writingyourvoice.org.uk

Bethany Rivers is also editor of the online poetry magazine, *As Above So Below,* which publishes poetry on the theme of spirituality and transcendence.

About Fly on the Wall Press:

A publisher with a conscience.
Publishing high quality anthologies on pressing issues, chapbooks and poetry products, from exceptional poets around the globe.
Founded in 2018 by founding editor, Isabelle Kenyon.

Other publications:

Please Hear What I'm Not Saying (February 2018. Anthology, profits to Mind.)
Persona Non Grata (October 2018. Anthology, profits to Shelter and Crisis Aid UK.)
Bad Mommy/Stay Mommy by Elisabeth Horan (May 2019. Chapbook.)
The Woman With An Owl Tattoo by Anne Walsh Donnelly (May 2019. Chapbook.)

Social Media:

@fly_press (Twitter)
@flyonthewall_poetry (Instagram)
@flyonthewallpoetry (Facebook)
www.flyonthewallpoetry.co.uk